Snow Resume
Nick Monks

Bluebell Publishing

For Amanda, Karl, Saskia

Credit: Cover image, Pexels credited to Pixabay

Title Page

Snow Resume- Nick Monks

Published June 2020

Printed June 2020

Printed by Lulu
www.lulu.com

ISBN:978-1-9163546-8-5

CONTENTS

Snow Resume

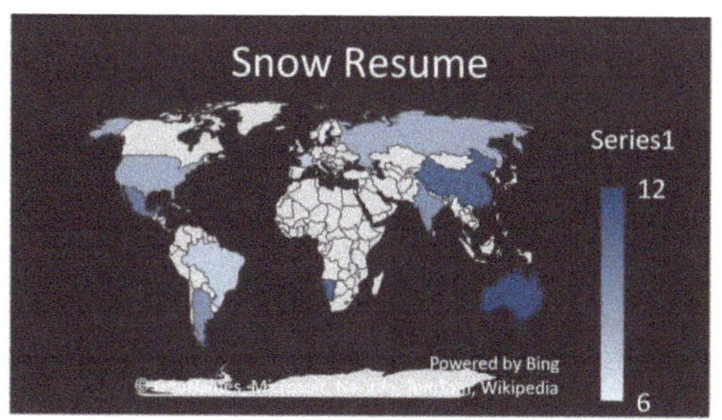

Snow 1

A carrier case of drill bits. A girl's nightclub handbag.
Making kitchen coffee. An empty coffee cup on the bedroom carpet
Absolute zero. The invasion of Februaries meandering night snow lanterns.
Three flickering stars whispering between glimpsed grey snow clouds.

Credit: Oleg Magni- Pexels

Snow 2

Terribly red and searingly hot. A red so vivid. Crocus petal-light wings. Descend through the sleeping night.

Snow 3

The ache/ the yearning/the striving/ the work
Crystalline fluttering baubles in a dark blue November sky.

Snow 4

Angled bread slanting in on a dying, tired, bent body

Snow medley in a sad minor key.

Snow 5

The white of snow is not white
It is absolute death. And absolute life. Utter aloneness.

Credit: Kristin Vogt- Pexels

Snow 6

Is a kettle broken, cracked, forlorn. In a nowhere kitchen
Then snow again. Here in Reykjavik.

Snow 7

Snow is not kind. Unendurable pain.

Snow 8

We hide in the magnolia temperate north.
Look at pictures in *National Geographic* magazine
While the washing machine talks. An ache on the side.
Extra saliva. An unexplained sharp leg pain
The door- bell chimes. The cooker is switched off after the
water has boiled. The pain foretold snow.

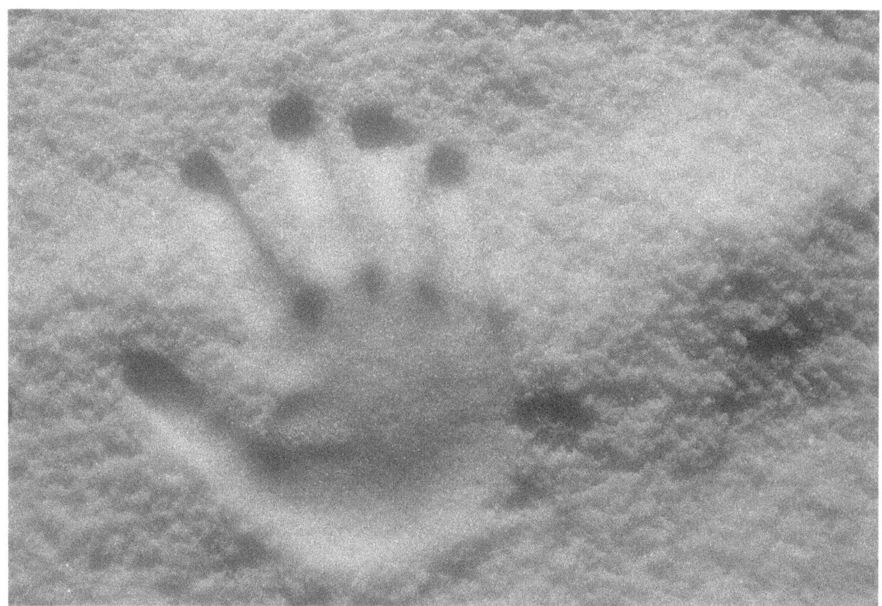
Credit: Matej- Pexels

Snow 9

Snow is kind to those in poverty, drug addicts, those in ruins. Snow understands and the pain is rendered null.

Snow 10

Snow though, has a social conscience
All these things inundated by snow fall again.

Credit - Pixabay

Snow 11

Is a blank forlorn face. So cold and blue. The smile is eternal.

Snow 12

The poet pens a last 3am poem
As snow covers lawns, street, drive, walls, roofs.

Snow 13

Terrible snow
Drinking the blood from your body
To refresh and ice render.

Snow 14

Snowed kissed- humble pauper/tramp
Crashed in a mire of snow jumble clothes
Wondering what to wear in winter-land

Snow 15

Cavernous hill. Swished peat covered curve
Of white against an alabaster grey sky.

Snow 16

Your neighbours reel around
In your absolute zero of a house
You sip melted crushed ice.
And clasp the sides of a car anti-freeze cannister
Air fans, three budget models on-
Third speed button on Christmas day
To complement the wished for snow- storms.

Credit: Pixabay

Snow 17

A kiss. So laden with purity and encompassed love
You will never recover
The delicate petals of snow meander fluttering.
In a deep blue night sky.

Snow 18

So terribly ice cold like wolfs teethe.

Snow 19

Ice jar on the windowsill
In the morning the flowers were dead
The water was solid ice
A forked thin crack on the vases side.

Ice Cubes in Tray 20

Lie like magic treasure boxes
In the cold dark top of the fridge
Waiting to peel across her pale skin
A torrent of summer folly.

Snow 21

Snow freezes bureaucracies making them ice cold
Like the fingertips of Rhiannon.

Snow 22

Becomes. Grows organically
Freezes pain. Is tender like a first love
Develops on the vine. Is slowness of realization
Is as patient as a glacier, or a spring season.

Credit: Pixabay

Snow 23

Ice white smile. Blank white land
As pure as the grimy city. -In the season of Rhiannon.

Snow 24

Terrible black snow of poverty
Indelible like white robes
On Boudicca in the blackness
Of a cold vigil in the trees in East Anglia.

Snow 25

Saliva and sweat and lymph fluid. But in a rare static white beauty.

St Petersburg Song 26

The river Neva is frozen now
The man lies on the snow road with starvations death blush
A hand grasp's at something. But there is nothing there-
But air. He imagines fir trees laden with snow.

Snow 27

Falls forever. A river. A mountain range. A distant city- scape. Towering fir forests.

Snow Medley 28

Majestic wonderland
Teethe bit
Joyesse elan
Overladen pines
Snow juice
Medley of snow fall
The grey river says stop
As silent wings cascade
On a man 8,000 miles from Fiona

Credit: Pixabay

Snow Medley 29

Peaks of mountains in the distance
So achingly blue
A mountain maid in red dress
Walks with poise and dignity across the tundra
Such wealth in the wind snow blizzard
Her dress wind tormented.

You have to sit. And marvel
At the snows equidistant sky fall
On the horizon the frozen far Northern sea
Stretching from the Russian tundra land

Credit: Flo Dahm- Pexels

Snow medley 30

Snow again. Honeyed grey sky
The abundance
A promise of treasure foretold
As the snows, snow fall on the snow plain
To be followed by mountain avalanche and death.

Nick Monks lives in Preston, Lancashire, UK. He studied Philosophy at Hull University. He has worked in scores of careers. He travelled widely for about seven years.

His poems have appeared in numerous UK magazines. And a few international. He is currently trying to write a novel and a filmscript.

www.ingramcontent.com/pod-product-compliance
Lightning Source LLC
LaVergne TN
LVHW052357100826
845147LV00013B/869

* 9 7 8 1 9 1 6 3 5 4 6 8 5 *